EMBRYOS & IDIOTS

TUPELO PRESS

Embryos & Idiots
Copyright © 2007 Larissa Szporluk

ISBN: 978-1-932195-52-1
Printed in Canada

First paperback edition
April 2007
Library of Congress Control Number: 2006908737

Tupelo Press
Post Office Box 539, Dorset, Vermont 05251
(802) 366-8185
www.tupelopress.org

Cover and book design by Josef Beery

EMBRYOS & IDIOTS

Henry,
Come to my
sheep farm!
(thanks for
listening)

LARISSA SZPORLUK

TABLE OF CONTENTS

I

II

III

Others came single; he who to be deemed
A god, leaped fondly into Etna flames,
Empedocles, and he who to enjoy
Plato's Elysium, leaped into the sea,
Cleombrotus, and many more too long,
Embryos and idiots, eremites and friars
White, black and grey, with all their trumpery.

Book III, ll. 469-75, *Paradise Lost*

I

Od is a mineral kingdom. Anoton
suspects his mother of breaking the law
against harboring plants and animals.
He reports her; she is demolished.
Anoton's father takes revenge. The boy's
head falls to Earth and becomes a small
mountain island. Millennia later, a girl
washes up on it. With the aid of a dog,
Anoton devours her.

Boulders

He knew she was hiding a bee. He could hear it
zapping inside her, trapped in the amber
nook that led to her mineral uterus.

He had been born with that sound,
the rain of maracas, maraud of a rose, and so lived
in his mind with a wax city, silver hives

of see-through honey, chambers crammed
with princess-waste and ice, and would be
almost crazy, brushing her outer stone,

of which he had grown enamored,
like a pilot of a bomb site, fingering the lever—
This century wants anything. Is that a soul?

Idol

Her organs were the resins of ancient pines,
rich with seeds and loess, fatal powders
of a lunatic faust, now-diseased meadows.
Anoton spilled the secret—wouldn't we all
to get what we want? He told the king
of her whewellite eyes, siliceous oozes,
horn-mad noises in her pelvic forest.
The king had her crushed, the loot handed
over in a moonstone box. But no matter how
hard Anoton shook, the bee was a silent
guest, a pressure point, a foil, a defiant sponge
that shriveled up in spite of what supplied it.

Pornography

Her rubble was displayed in the royal
courtyard in cases labeled animal
and vegetable-corrupted. Her brain,
in a flask of boric acid, zithered the air
like luciferin, a glowing warning.

When Anoton came, he sized her up
with equal parts of severed feeling,
relieved to note her mental dwindling.
Then out she went — in clouds of white.
It was his first and finest blanket.

Reaper

His father stepped out in full obsidian splendor
and swung. "Papa!" The head flew off
like a petrified stork, up through the roofless
house and out of the belt of metallic cloud
that kept the stone race bound, and flew
like liberation through the cold infinitude
that expands inside the living like a cache
of eggs. Does it matter what we're made of?
A grain unfolds, the sun, the same, making
gold of morning. The facts then change: gold
is bad, the sun is pain, the malt, black rot,
and all that faith gets cut from our first story.

Ignoramus

We are held to death like the knife
to the objective, mistaking the objective,
ever missing, except once. Anoton
was just a boy, and just his head — giant clod
of blistered jade — was falling fast to Earth
with the loud whist of a gas flame
colliding with a liquid proof. Eternal life
is nonsense. We who are old and full of words
consent to disappear. Anoton did not.
He hit the base of an unfished sky and lay,
a numb grenade, gummed with strombs
whose stomachs pulsed and slavered.

Painfully Aware

In a time when slaves were all named Bark,
the mountain was a vast erection of mysterious

garbage. And Bark? Did he really live in a house
made of hair, and soothe the cries of frozen stars,

and wander in accordance with the wind,
lapped in a sea of ewes? Who had he been

before he was stolen, beaten with bells, twisted
like dough? Bark read the future in bones

and rinds, knew when the dragon above him
was smoking, that the smoke made him high,

like a root poking out of the night's coat,
venomous and stopless. But then his native

hunch perished in the lightning, and the one great
thing that egged him on, like pharaoh's boat,

flattened out, and what fried sap, like our whole
love, or eels that mate with raindrops.

Orientation

The head slept. Only near the end
of humans did it leave oblivion
enough to learn that its once-smooth
chin was barbed with medicinal
life, hellebore, vomica, ginger,
that its jaw to the clouds was wide
with its last said word,
and the eyes, though fogged, could sense
the touch-and-go of the domino
waves, increasing steps on its face
of things that were hungry
that had always been awake,
rooting out instars, gathering dates,
magnifying screw-worms
in their tertiary stage, or wrapping up
a manhunt in a mangrove glade
and the compromising posture
of a cleaned-out leg
that just the other summer
jumped in every game, and suddenly
it understood the twinkling.

Passive-Aggressive Music

Crests breaking over his severed neck
dumped salt on his lips and the salt
formed cakes like infected sores.
In time, the cakes became domes,
and gulls set their nests in the dome
umbrellas. But during the midday
summer sun, even the shade there
shone, like Judas' eyes on the fish
at supper. He never wondered where
his body was. He only murmured
to the gull who seemed to know him
something about his mother's pitch,
the sharp injustice of its softness,
and what's so important that it makes
you forget, like ammonia, everything?

Naves and Navels

The sea is the greatest mother.
Even now that we know she is finite and dirty,
we still come back to her rim, admitting
we still belong there, like those to the church
when it's time to be joyfully married,
assured by an airtight seal.

The night the girl was hurled
onto the mountain, the sky was a pulverized
rose. There were walls in the air,
pink, trembling spires. Did Anoton know?
Does anyone know? We who are old
and full of words?

The gardens of Od had no flowers. Call it
the spell of perfume. It takes the wind
of our breath to float a paper boat,
and the damage that follows is real. "The king
has long ears; the king has long ears."
It echoes. We know.

Weavers

In the late afternoon when the thrust
of the waves turns violet,
Anoton's violets wave. That's how the shade

of her hair is decided.
That her eyes are pins of stars
he is told by the gull—

because he has to know, has to ask,
because the place in his ear
where she lies is phonolithic

and the sound that it makes when her body
stirs jolts him like existence.
He tries to shy away, but can't raise his head

from the ocean bottom. Can you weave
if you are woven?
Can you drown if you are stone?

Is wind your only supper?
Does it scarf your mouth, loud with wolf,
or hem-and-haw, like maidenhood?

Accessory

Things breed in the bath
of Anoton's mouth the world
has never seen: worms with plumes,
newt-like ghouls, armadillo
boas. As the gull describes the girl
over and over, his floor grows warm
with flaming sugar. Can we
avoid the misadventure?
Is it seductive to obey?

The gull, whose name is Mara,
swoops without warning and pulls a tuft
of the sleeping girl's hair.

The girl doesn't cry, only probes the spot
in a state of wonder. The skins
of the moon are exposed when we behold it;
we call the bloodless bruises *seas*.
Falling apart is like going undercover —
we drop our sunny side
to meet the dirt,

then loiter there, eyelids halfway
closed, no longer certain
if the disarray down our face
and neck is ours or theirs.

Stalactite Habit

Mara drags the hair across Anoton's lips for hours.
The hair swishes. His surface
ripples like the all-knowing muscle of a horse.

He asks to feel it in his throat.
Noodles of drool
coil on the topaz water. Balanced on a tooth

formation, mid-mouth down, Mara drops it.
He asks for more. Mara pauses. He asks for more.
These are the hesitations

that make us who we are, mark us for the haul:
No, the oldest word in the vainest circle.
Yes, the promise that burns,

mathematically tapers, banks on its slick
like biblical siblings:
Yes, we will serve you, and mock

the just sun. Yes, we will put
our trust in your shadow. Yes, yes,
and dress all your longings, and relish your bite.

S.O.S

The girl was scooping clams
when the gull pulled a switchblade
lunge. Instead of hair,
the beak took a cube of flesh.

Mara shut her eyes,
flew dutifully back, the catch now akin
to a cherry. Why is the worst
the only certainty?

Anoton didn't thank her,
just sucked and sucked
until it must have changed from red
to paraffin by morning.

The sweet rubber of everything.
Why did Mara do it,
appoint her home her master?
We are orphans. We have never

had a father in the sky.
The earth and the water will leave us,
but oxygen first, and away
like a gasp went Mara,

mean as the arrow
her soul had become, deserting her young
to yell unto no one.
We must get out of this infancy.

It isn't erotic. The smile no longer
moves us, only the loathing,
and that by itself
makes a dangerous papoose.

Transubstantiation

Anoton gave orders.
The mutt of history listened,
or whatever it was, monarchy's
harpy, then bounded down the cliff
on cloven fours.

When it reached the beach,
the girl was leaning on a shoulder.
(As soon as he had stabbed her,
Achilles raped her — Penthesilea, the soldier,
lifeless in her breastplate.)

Smoke is *lacrimosus*.
In smoke and in tears, ecstasy
bristles, like the paunch of an ostrich
under a livid sword —
a swill that swells with accusation.

When the dog bared its teeth,
froth breaking forth,
the shoulder vanished. It must have been
an angel's. A human would have
stayed, at least to seem to save her.

Pecuniary

It seized her by the waist
and ran, her dangling head
bashing the rocks,

the rocks bashing back.
At the top, abrupt silence —
like a dropped baton.

What better rush
than an urge served fresh,
the girl's brief story

scrolled up tight, a Persian rug,
the blood at rest,
a pervert's inertial toy?

What does a whippet imagine?
What could a trophy
mean to an Arabian?

We love this preposterous
quest. When it nudges her
into the pit, her body clinks,

an exhausted bauble,
rolls down the walls
of the buyer's yawn,

his wholesale gulp,
her edible cunt,
an optimum bargain.

Twilight Wedge

Black flowers rise from the slime.
She is his branch now,
his outcry.
When we glance from east
to west, the gravity
of ransom — a swoosh through a dark
blue mesh, our only sun
a drawn-out question.
Are you deep inside yourself or not?
Are you a moron with a rock?
Can you push your intuition,
take your house apart
in one brute swipe,
pry it from its moorings,
like a shearer the entire
wardrobe of a sheep?
Can you love what isn't lovely,
crack your locks,
enter bravely,
face the defaced meat?
Psychic doorknobs tumble out:
the devil's seven brothers;
the lord's gold stars.
Gather them like mushrooms.
Screw them when you're frightened.
Lose sight and then you'll see
how glorious the gore is,
and you'll kneel to it,

you heathen,
and the night will bleat,
no doubt.

Victorious Female

Victorious how? Anoton's
mind grows spastic.
Olive trees snarl the hill.

Rams with curved horns
batter each other, deranged
by bubbling groins.

Sperm splashes the pampas,
mist of aborted rainbows.
Just to exist is criminal.

His breezes go cyclone,
coastlines discordant as ever.
He longs for permanent

burial. *Where is my therapy?*
Schism, fulfillment.
He's Venus's son.

He stomachs her love,
vomits her silver pajamas
and goblets. It cannot

be tallied, this theatre
of war. She tweets
every morning, unhinges

her box, offers him
oranges, puddings, abalone
guns that don't cock.

Dark Eros

She smirks, sets herself up
on a cinder cone — How does
it feel, she asks the old mountain,
to have no choice but to feel?
Succuss of Anoton's glottis.
Rumbles, plutonic debris.
Feel this, she hisses into his
sphincter, then does something
evil with fruit — oh, the power
to cry! Oh, to be able to cry!
His mouth is under the sea now.
The past is a quasi-fetish.
I was only a child, but my
obsession with you was divine.

II

Everything starts talking: Anoton's maker,
a cuckoo bird, a condemned man, a recluse,
a mental patient, a tyrant, a seed, a god,
a saint, a knight, a virgin...

"All th' unaccomplished works of Nature's hand,
Abortive, monstrous, or unkindly mixed,
Dissolved on earth, fleet hither, and in vain,
Till final dissolution, wander here."

Book III, ll. 455-58, *Paradise Lost*

Apocalypse Pie

This sea of shit,
of fishy shit, the only fish
the sapiens left,
fills the stony hero's
nose, the few low dells,
all overbuilt —
the wind saws through,
a wasp or two, the bloody
buzz of function-lust,
but all that's lost,
the end is near, the earth's
a pear, we gnawed it up,
but what's that tail,
way up there, it's sort
of white, a crust
of light, but awfully
thick, a shroud of spit,
it could have shut
the piper up, or did it
exit from his flute,
translucent shit,
enchanted tunes, but who
can pipe, the hero's
stone, no one flouts,
they've all been drowned,
the hero too, so no one's
here, but who is he

but part of me, the part
that's stone, that's breaking
down inside this sea
but feels the tail, the tail
is soft, it wants to help
lift me out, but who
am I — my God, it's time,
the tail is time, it wants
it back, the past,
the plague, it wants
to save those hophead
rats that danced away,
plunked into their river
grave, its long blue
tail, the children too,
whose little town
let them down,
saved a bag of gold
or two, saved — my God,
I hear it now, the hymn
they heard, it's true,
it's great, it makes me
want to bow out too,
but God, it's her, my
mom, for me, reaching
down, for me, her son,

who loves too much
her long blue arm,
my mom, my God,
who serves me now
a crow, it seems, to eat,
it seems, eat crow,
she squeaks, her silver
fork sinking through,
a prick or two, to make
cocksure I'm stuffed.

Ecstatic Technique

It was a racial suicide.
Day after day, millions of walls
were erected. Homes doubled
in height. We were the empire
builders. We gave wings
to our cellars, pillars to porches.
We mowed and we plowed
our dominion over, lit chamomile
meadows on chemical fire,
buried our dogs alive in the slag,
their shag poking up
like so many throw rugs. I slept
with the wrong person first,
lay in my blood like a childhood
raincoat. We and our shamans.
We and our cannibal values.
We, our ridiculous hopes.
Anoton? I think you already know.
He stopped living for me.
He was nonsense in a non-place.
The girl he stalked and swallowed?
She had stood for his soul,
but couldn't uphold him;
a lesser Atlas, she threw in
the towel, the wild blue yonder,
is sprawled on his cheek now
in a ruby bikini, for the rest
of the story, which is practically
over, like an unlucky jelly,
drying right up as we speak.

Cuckoo

I nudge the eggs
of not my make,
watch them drop
without a thought —
dead who? dead who?
Who cares? They're
not my make. I'm
cuckoo-true, a blood
and thunder freedom
monger — *free what?*
from who? Free you,
my boy, from mama
bird and birdie wife
and future brood.
You're free to crack,
to stink, to cook.
You're better off off
the hook, and off
the clock of my off-war
where time is space
and space is time
and both are wound
to wind up mine —
without a wall, what
can hang? Without
the sky, why not fall?
It's all all off, but
I'm in tune. Death
is math. Rest assured
the nest left you.

Stars and Marrow

Mother, it's raining little stones
like dark gray caramels, like
tumbling playing dice that clamor
for my soul, but not the one
you gave me. I was whisked
into the midnight of my making,
like a cake for a whoring queen,
a bloody Aceldama. At last
the boxes of the world's final zoo
are finally quiet. No more rhyming
apes, no how's and why's of herring
hearing, just the agonizing dial
of the diatonic sloth. I turned
my back on you and died like a duck
in the open, a pile of yesterday's
nobody's child. Strapped to my high
yellow chair, the waves that lunged
at me were carnal, but no, I didn't
mind. There is so much good
in the worst of us, so much bad
in the best. I found succor in the devil
when the angels cooked my head.

The Recluse

Light rose like a bee in the early
watery twirl of the bird. In her bath,
my rosewater daughter screamed
and twirled without feeling grief.
Like the moon, she could mate
with the first early bird or the bee's
first mate, and twirl like wool,
razed too deep, my daughter,
that sheep, my grief, her watery
mate in the heat, her early-bird
scream in the moon's rose-twirl,
her youth as she bathes in the light
of my hate, like a bee without feeling
its feet, or me, my grief at losing
my youth in the loom of the scream
that spooled me out like a fledgling
kite from my heavenly term in hell's
cocoon, and followed me down
with watery teeth, and gnawed my
hide until I was too weak, to stop her,
my daughter, from parting my walls,
grazing my brain like a thorn.

Mr. Punishment

He took my stack of punk,
pound by pound. What else
did the nightbird borrow?
The whistle of the wind,
its phantom radar, *mama*,
the organum of all language.
I've never been this cold.
I'm in the middle of an island,
doctor. I have one begonia,
had to dome it like my own
vagina—you know he pecked
the moon, stone by stone,
to build himself a moonstone
cradle? You notice there's
no tide? You notice nothing
howls now—nothing's left
to blame them on, lunatics,
nothing wanes or waxes
new. He just scratches
at my frozenness, like you,
my mental hold, to see
if I'm obedient, a pigeon
for a whim, a classical good
daughter, numb to her nude
groom. So don't pretend
it matters whether I am him
or he is you, his omnipotence
the affect or the galaxies
he raids—tap into my riddle
and we all go down the drain.

Cold and Cowed

On the night of the long knives,
a clown set about
murdering his loved ones — *you, you, you,*
for the little thing you did,
way back when, to shame me.
They were buried upside-down,
dangling in the canopies
of musty coke, corrupted ferns, sunlit lands
of long ago. Look out for the clown
whose heart is brown and boiled.
His phantom ruling passion,
a bladdery canary,
plays her hired ditty
on the cherry of his nose,
stinging, clanging, clinging drips
that drum his tongue
which stands straight up
and bats them — *you, you, you,*
for being dead and coming back.
Look out for the clown
who splits all sides
with cutlery, obscenity, chicanery,
whose circus tents are wombs
he rents. Shadow him
when he goes in and turns the herd
to gravy — *you, you, you,*
stir the bung and mum your curse:
munchkin stink-pot has-been. But who are you
who holds the spoon?
Little Devil Doubt, a member of his set.

Asleep in the Seed

Shhh. Stay down.
Don't wake yourself up.
Stay closed as a toad
in its winter funk
of mummified pus
and sediment guck.
Commit your form
to this coffinous gloom
where the albino sun
moonlights as onion.
Your brow will slop off
when the new one is born,
a gleaming new organ,
plain as a shawl. Stay
down. That axis to virtue—
all wrong, all wrong.
A mouse builds a house
with imaginal powers,
bloomed mental flowers,
wheels of blue cheese.
The skull of a heifer
harbors a goldfish,
the thing she was fixed on
last and most. It was
going to hurt you, the future
informs us, wring out
your juices, a crepe-paper

pupa. Stay down.
Forget her, forget him.
Stay smothered, uncoded,
unaltered by age.
Love freely in storage.
Get pregnant while dormant.
Lie in your throat
through your teeth.

Trinity

You were two people,
the sun and the moon,
action, reflection,
superficial, profound.
You lived in each other,
poles of each other,
exalted each other,
vampirely. Then you
were puerile, locked
in a bamboo cabana.
Along came a brown
maroon cloud: cinders,
aerosol, fuel, coming to
burn your burning-hot
room. Like the mood
of the lord, the chief
of your tribe, the first
to deflower, a tireless
fountain, bionic arrival,
it blew back your back,
ripped out your middle,
fathered your cancer,
tripled your person,
dirtied the world —
don't you remember?
Then cut off your hands
once they could juggle,

like ducks on the water,
blind to the blind,
and conjured the ghost
that now you resemble.

Celestial Militia

All my little boy wants
is a whipping. Oh,
and maybe some ice
in a glass of his urine,
or maybe a ride in the jaws
of an oily dragon,
or maybe he wants
to waste all his time
on detachment, un-darn a sock,
suck his own dick
down to a droplet.
If all that's the case,
he'll still go to heaven;
he's all-around good,
like Joan the old scarecrow,
Saint Joan of Arc,
bending and yelling,
spitting up embers
at on-coming peckers,
who scares me, her goodness,
like his does, my son's,
who does all my feeling,
my bleeding and feeling,
does it all for me,
who steals my deep life
like a gunshot at sunset,
and leaves me in clearings,
a radiant dud.

Participation Mystique

Who called my name,
called it wrong, called me
Joan, called me dull,
brushed me hard, struck
a match, lit me up,
hummed a bar, dropped
his pants, fanned the flames,
lost his stars, splashed
my face, left me dead,
female saint, in the cave,
unreclaimed? Who
slipped away, shed his myth,
not a god, not a knight,
just a john stuck in time,
jacking off, cock in palm,
in the zone, drumming on,
eyes agog with tristesse
for the come he sees go
droning back through his
hole — a musical tease,
like whales with humps
who teach their pups
to seem to sing: be blue,
be proud, be rare as
spice, do naught for free,
bare your lock but hide
the key, be the line between
all things — the war for
peace, the offbeat beat,
the twilight wall that falls
on youth, the pent-up creep
betrothed to truth.

Galloping Motif

Hear this! Hear this! Mass is not an obstacle.
It is equally a nothing. You can restore
your mother's voice by toying gallantly
with water. A unity machine can wheel
the tumor of her body into flakes of cosmic
snow that will cover the whole garden,
the ladybugs, madonna. The universe is forked
like the tails of yellow tuna, more and more
good fortune. There's a horse for you,
a hot-blood. You can ride it to her heart.
The valves are locked? Just giddy-up,
don't waste time on manners. If someone's
lurking in her arteries, a trumpeter, a wanderer,
a wrinkled general from space, remember
this: he cuckolded your dad, tore her brocade
curtain. A bone to pick? I should think.
Trample him, but hurry. Your steed is losing
parts. *Starry starry lifetime.* Serpentine at canter,
then a flying change of lead, then cast a spell
on her last breast and penetrate that dragon.

Everlastings

Don Giovanni
seduces eternity.
He's after the woman,
the absolute woman,
not just her parts.
I was pet like a dog
in a dark garage
by a children's doctor.
But what are the really important questions?
Monkeys? Technology?
These new hamsters
made of motors and fleece
curl up at the rape victim's feet.
It can't be emotion. No one is higher
than their time. Today,
if you crush the sweet rabbits,
they smell like tobacco;
their pistils are beige and wool.
Or so said the weed guide
who rogued all the pussies
and asters. No, he wasn't a prince,
and it was more of a dump
than a pasture. Fragments of a statue
of a damsel, early medieval,
were forced back together
with chivalrous eros
for one last act.
When the spirit takes its leave,

the sensuous, freed of god,
with dirty artsy hands,
works its giant talent
unabashed.

III

Anoton expresses remorse, but it is
impotent remorse. He learns from the
voices that there is no grace. The only
fall is from our bodies into the mind,
into that "Limbo large and broad,
since called/The Paradise of Fools, to
few unknown."

Book III, II, 495-96, *Paradise Lost*

I, Anoton

I in the torso
lying on the floor
with my mourning
dad. I in the finding
that I am not restricted
to my lithic head.
I in the vulture
who circles the future.
I in the wide
open field of reform.
I in the gnome
alone on the seesaw,
always the low end,
squatter for hope.
I and my birdie
bride in a furrow
of a burnt winter coat
of a nobody soldier.
I in my carriage,
immaculate newborn,
safe from the knowledge
that I would expand
in poundage and
damage, that mother
could shift from
comforting lifter
to object to possibly

terribly conquer—
I in the useless
sorry that haunts me
like a napkin of snow
laundered in April,
caught by the water
as if by an eyeball,
an intimate witness
to thin-skinned nature.
Who would believe
such a fancy flirtation,
such feathery radii,
could leave any imprint?
A boy made of stone
is harder to pardon.
So why do you bother,
father, to hold my
cold body and cry?

The Usual Cadaver

We fell to Earth with Lucifer.
We crossed the sun
the whole way down.
You would have thought
that we were cranes,
or crows of unholy dimensions,
or a form of UFO
flashing like a carousel,
warning you against us.
But we landed short, or more like
dumb, on ears of corn,
not worth their names,
nor you, worth yours, your head
a gourd of senseless sinew.
What is left to say?
We are adding something gloomy
to the jewelry water,
a tinge to the blossom rains.
To the oneness of allness,
an especial time, especial place—
a juvenile smile
to carve in you and claim.
In the spirit of the whipper,
we wish you picture-perfect pain.

Gospel of the Mean

No one gives a damn about your music.
A dog and a duck grew lustful.
That's you. That's who you are.

They birthed such an eerie baby, you,
who you are, of Labrador fur
and rough orange feet, screaming the news

in a screwed-up language. Lusts.
Do giraffes covet wives?
Do their necks keep their lusts way up,

up like the stone time threw up
to form Mount Olympus? Lusts.
It must be the brain that does this.

Metaphors. Neighbors. Dogs licked Ahab's
blood, blood is the body's river,
the Yangtze, the Yellow, dragging the soil

of China into an orgy of fins.
Cain fell. Cain was restored. Lusts.
You should have shut up

when you were still young,
spent more time chewing tall leaves.
Or laying way low, like a lizard on granite,

licking the dust your mother
kicked up, long before dogs and songs
about long bad water and kings.

Shape-Shifter

You should just die, old snake,
everything's old, you know, nobody

cares, not now, see how they nod,
dead leaves, over your old smashed

face, isn't it nice, this shush, it was
enough, your life, why do you stir,

dead sir, why does your tongue still
jump, there is no sun, not now,

you were a boy, yes, once, boy
on a witch-hunt high, now you can

flop, old fetch, drop like a dog, old
stench, lie with your bark dry-baked,

death is its own good crowd, death
listens hard, old bard, you had an ear,

yes, once, ear for a dirge, old worm,
sang on your mom, no qualm, are you

redeemed, bad seed, I would say not,
headcheese, your halo is low, it seems,

the lamp of a swamp, old leech, fungus
and gas, dung heap, not of His Grace,

dead beat, too nicked to speak, indeed,
fear is its own safe crowd, just let it

out, old fart, shit is the one straight
art, that's what it takes, old mouth,

shit that can sing a brick house to its feet,
wing the dead breeze, bring back

the birds with a load of its cheep—
eat shit and shit green and keep quiet.

Freak of Luck

I was there at the beginning of the world.
He made me with a wave of his hand.
His hand was clean. His geese were clean.

His rain came down on everything: the unicorn,
the forester, the earthworm. God made
the unicorn sad. God dropped his son in the sand.

God was a lush. The sun rose up. I rose up.
I cleaned all the cities. I can't tell a story. The truth
isn't pretty. God made white people boring,

then yawned and they all turned to stone.
I was a poisonous hairy. Pity he didn't spare me.
I was good for the fear and the dog-eared loner.

Only the honeycomb moray, holed away in a cove,
managed to rear her one cold egg. How do I
know this? The newborn's a reborn; every

beloved is the same: the chosen, the corn son,
the phallus unhusked—I'm back in the palace.
It's springtime. Fags mop my blood.

The Man in the Moon

The man in the moon looks out
of the moon, looks out of the moon
and says, "I live in a criminal
woman." A cockatiel snores,
a drape on its cage, a jungle
of two-way mirrors. Nay,
there's a low, low feeling
shoeing its way through the snow.
It looks like a lady, is fuzzed
like a buck, lets everyone
suck her, plays everyone's
mother, is here to condone
our long life of cake. The man
in the moon looks out of the moon
again. "Does it get more disgusting?"
Nay. He spits on his fingers,
holds them out to the sun.
The last day of Socrates. It *is*
about men, their pleasure and pain,
object, desire, that two-headed
twin. Nay, it's them teeth
that washed up that give me
the willies, teeth of a billion bison.
So many things we done killed
in our rush to awaken. But marry,
how much less of a mayhem
had we just stayed in bed.

Dispersion

Running away from snow, the snow itself,
the chaser. Dirty rainbows, horny
faces, ripping out of prisms—

dinosaurs no larger than a chicken;
others who shook the Earth. All children
love them, love their stupid death,

how their breath puffed out in blossoms
as they charged and sank and yelped,
then turned and churned, with ferns and dirt,

an era here, an era there, all carbon, coal,
the grossest flesh to scorch in hell.
Later, as uranium, they're daughtered

into missiles, sometimes really pretty ones,
no hard feelings, and forced to bake a star,
or firework a creek, or leave a squishy

tooth to commemorate the warmth
deadliness affords them, or weep like Job
and mow the grass with patience.

Ponderer

I know
that my pond
knows what a fern
is, knows too
what fronds do —
hart's tongue
wrapped Adam,
stag horn rode
Eve, and my pond
knows the first
girls to walk Earth
were long-haired
and shocking,
stepped out of ribs
like miniature
rockets, and I know
my pond knows
that ribs can stick
out, drip like
slim candles,
like some boys
I know who slip
into otters, whose
pelts come loose
from love at all
hours. My pond
answers dryness
in gallons of sperm,
knows that I rip
and I think

only of ferns.
Though our slug
is our god, our
boneless ankle,
who crosses the
surface by hoping
and clinging,
one day he'll drop
out of sight
like an earring
and limbo
without him and just
us will break,
and hell will be
founded on heavenly
guilt, for I am as
guilty as you who
looks in, sees
that I'm swollen
with every freak
thing—free-floating
fingers and fingerless
hands caught in the
storm of the scum
that I am.

Judges

There is nothing beautiful about us.
We are not the Okapi (legs of a zebra,
gait of giraffe, prehistoric muzzle,
heart strong as wood, whose home
was where its bed was, or might be).
No. We are not. We are stumped
like our forests. We stomp into deserts
like drunken chameleons, gas every
cubit, call it defensive, then graze
on the still-growing hair of the grave
yard, manes long as Samson's — Samuel!
God's gift to Hannah! Samson! Flim
flammed by whores, their slippery
feelings, sweet-water whispers, bosomy
sponges. I know a Sam. We all know
a Sam. I have a son. His name isn't Sam,
but he's the nicest paleontologist.
He's after a carcass the color of breast
milk, a particular femur, longitudinal
sliver, has another thing coming that isn't
so precious — that our quest should deceive
us, hood our good eyes, tip the seesaw
of peacetime! Shame on the zealous
and jealous. Shame on the half-fish god
who dined on himself and survived.

Metallurgy

The simultaneity of styles
increases the confusion of the form.
We are like the moribunds.
We grope ourselves,
accelerate our impotence,
animate our manias,
throw pennies in the wish-pond,
wish for better wish-ponds,
deify our clothes. Time and breath
have inter-grown so much
that our skeletons are gasping
on an insubstantial floor.
Around and around we go,
prey to grim relationships:
a snow-white vein, a whalebone
ouch, ashamed to say
we've scraped the depths,
made molehills out of mountains.
And now this sunken corridor,
like a girlhood that expired,
the natural tattoo inside her vision
an aggregate of dots
the rock hound blinded,
his incandescent shovel, from her
mortal puddle, coming up
loaded with old iron hat:
How the will-power willows
in the molten summer.

Chatoyancy

Why be born, witch,
to just destroy, witch,
coat the eyes, witch,
with terror, do you know?
I watched them fuss,
witch, against your tit,
witch, this very morning,
for a hold. Not just cats,
witch, but lambs, witch,
and man, witch, every
heaving lung that cries
for more — it's just a fact,
witch, that we're all
damned, witch, to fall
for what is fiend and fast
and hung most glossed
and high, what crosses
stars and disembogues
and goads our bloated
pride, like the fact, witch,
your crystal ball, witch,
saw itself, inside itself,
drenched like common
stone, and that means
you, witch, and me,
witch, and them, witch,
this entire farm, awash.
So what's your loss,
witch? Let it out, witch,
which of us your spigots

will miss most, which
animal without whose
grip your mams will
pout and callous. Not that
runt, witch, whose tips,
witch, would slice them
off like roses — tell me
it's not him. He won't
latch on. He hates your
guts. He'll swell you out,
do us in. We'll drown in
milk along with him — that's
your bliss? To die with him?
Witch, that rat can swim.

Democratic Ghosts

It was sad to be between four walls.
The wind brought odors of moss, chanterelles,
cantos of owls. *Where is my therapy?*

The hands that reached for him were branches,
extensions of his fickle parents.
Death was horrible because death was possible.

Arms tore the shingles from his only roof,
pounded his turtle. *My gazelle, my little birdie*
of the forest. Lalala. They loved him.

The truth is indestructible. They loved him.
They entered his hut, provided the guests,
the crumb-cakes, then slept in a row, all together,

like a tin of sardines, teenage hookers, brains
off-kilter, and they were warmer there
than anywhere they knew of in his nightmare.

Abraham's Bosom

Think of the frog
in its refuge of blue
that holds the whole sky
in its stink of a cheek,
which is not unlike man
in his sanctum of mind
who seldom forgets
to seldom unwind,
who chirps out his kinks
like a blockbuster clock,
walled in the thing
that is smaller than him,
but only in size.
Think of the floating
heart in the bog land,
its compound of petals,
seduced by indefinite
knots, not unlike clouds
that nibble our thoughts
like squirrels their nuts,
robbing our skulls
of their last conscious
seconds—we won't enter
heaven. We've never
been tried. It all happened
on us, not to us, like
moonlight, like cuckoos.
We echoed, reflected,
banked on good health,

but when push came to
shove, and shove edged us
over the bluff, we blew
up like zephyrs, and lifted
ourselves, and we sailed,
unassailed, but we still
aren't at rest.

Mother-of-Pearl Clouds

Let's call on the plasmoids
to splotch up their picnic.
Let's snow ultraviolet
so they grow extra limbs.
Let's give vegetables sex lives,
grill them flagrante.
Let's unite the divided
so the shy one crawls back
to his witch, so his witch
can flog him till sunrise.
Let's be lenticular, delicate.
Let's stretch over Norway.
Let's terrorize swing-sets,
yank down some knee-socks,
fondle some calves.
Let's cause some traumata.
Let's hide all their gods.
Let's extend civil twilight,
rattle a private, scour
and wax it. Let's not let them
think we're just passing.

Grin and Bear

Had we been forty lambs and made
that same jeer, and not forty boys,
we still would have died killed,
and the road would have thickened
just as grotesquely, with clots, and fleece
too, and the god-summoned she-bear,
mouth full of mutton, might have produced
a less Hebrew sound, not retched as
much as relished the baa, and not hustled
off, but danced in the massacre, and the truth,
that we can't fix our littleness, *that*
would have cut loose, slipped like a cloak
atop the invisible — Elisha, seer, it's true.
You're bald as a pumpkin, a fruit bat,
a scrotum. You can't not see it. It's blatant.
We laugh. We'll die if we don't if we do.
See, we mean to be mean to be mean,
for what would the good of being mauled
for being good be? Of a chirp if a bird
didn't lust, of an unbloody rebuttal
to an insult or two or forty? None. It's
the tension we're after, isn't it, E.? The grit
and the screams and the post-mortem
powder, your name in the bible, our sauce
scatting out of a wild she-asshole.

Terminus

My dog barks
at a part
moon. Why
choose?

I moon
the dark,
bog my part.

My head
is in a
stronghold
the morning after
drugs. My
overalls are
satin. I'm climbing
a tall machine.

On the panel,
I push every single
candy-coated
button. That's who
I was then —
mental druid
nomad
leaking luck.

In the mew
of noon,

I park my hawk,
my hark of ache.

My dog comes back,
his saucer-eyes.
He chews my hips
like tar and yaps:

The war's in your ears.
The war's in your shoes.

When I blow myself,
I hold myself.
The whole place
stammers —

The war's in your cadaver.
The war's your ever-after.

Dog, there's no one left.
Just straw
and smoke
and lost control —
my shallow soul
at home at last.

Satan at Length

A warm west harbinger wind
knocks the caterpillars
off the candelabra
of my hollow olive tree. I yawn
in the softening tufa. I yawn
and yawn as they fall
through my jaw like toweled
newborns. Infinity,
what a goose you are.
I yawn at the steely blueness
of the thousand dusky snakes
that make the sky a snaky place,
yawn at the sweetness
of rising late, deadly bored
with my deadly labor. I crawl
over cucumbers, radish.
See how I whip the vicious grist
of the august steppe, en route
to the Ark, yawning, yawning?
I dream of the seaside,
of the lone ravine of my own
dead yawn, like a room
with nobody else, and I know
why I'm last in line,
after the cattle. I'm firm
as the plunger the plumber pumps
to unclog our kingdom

of memory's crud. I come in
handy, without meaning
much, like a happily-ever-after,
or a belch of trust.

ACKNOWLEDGMENTS

American Poetry Review "Dark Eros"

Black Warrior Review "Mr. Punishment," "Mother-of-Pearl Clouds"

Bat City Review "Cuckoo"

Black Clock "Celestial Militia"

Columbia Poetry Review "Satan at Length (The Yawning Snake),"
"Gospel of the Mean"

Cream City Review "Chatoyancy"

Faultline "Anoton Od" (Boulders, Idol, Pornography, Reaper, Ignoramus,
Orientation, Passive-Aggressive Music, Naves and Navels);
"Freak of Luck," "The Man in the Moon," "Apocalypse Pie"

Hayden's Ferry Review "Shape-Shifter," "Ponderer"

Hotel Amerika "Painfully Aware," "Democratic Ghosts"

The Journal "Dispersion"

Kalliope "Trinity," "Metallurgy"

Margie "Judges," "Grin and Bear"

McSweeney's Quarterly Concern "The Recluse" (reprinted)

The National Poetry Review "Terminus"

Now Culture "Stars and Marrow," "Galloping Motif"

Parlorgames "Weavers," "Accessory," "S.O.S.," "Stalactite Habit"

Perihelion "Pecuniary," "The Usual Cadaver"

Portland Review "Ecstatic Technique," "Participation Mystique"

Salt Hill "Victorious Female," "The Recluse," "Moral Stillness"

Stride Magazine "Twilight Wedge," "Asleep in the Seed,"
"Abraham's Bosom," "Cold and Cowed"

**NATIONAL
ENDOWMENT
FOR THE ARTS**

Supported in part by an award from
the National Endowment for the Arts and
a grant from the Ohio Arts Council.